Dancing
Around the World

By Nicolas Brasch

CELEBRATION PRESS
Pearson Learning Group

Contents

Dancing Around the World

Start tapping your feet, and get ready to move. We are going dancing around the world. People dance for all sorts of reasons. They dance to celebrate an event or to entertain an audience. People tell stories and express emotions through dance. Sometimes people dance simply to enjoy themselves.

Let's take a closer look at a few dances. The dances come from many places. As you read, look for the different roles dance plays in different countries.

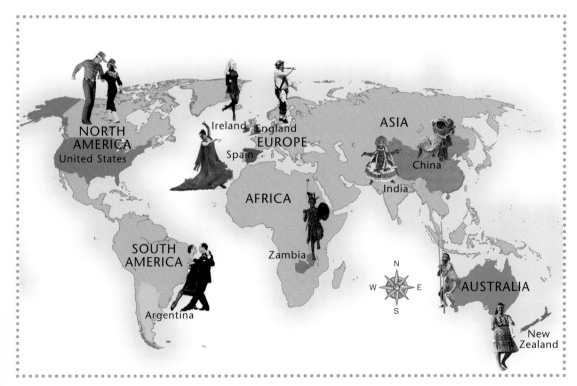

People do different dances throughout the world.

Asia

Kathakali Dance of India

Our journey begins in India, home of a dance called kathakali (KUT-uh-KUHL-ee). The word *kathakali* means "story-play." The dance began in the 1600s. Today, it is performed at theaters.

This dance tells stories through movement, expressions, and gestures. Kathakali dancers act out stories from two famous Indian poems, the *Ramayana* (ruh-MY-yuh-nuh) and the *Mahabharata* (MAH-huh-BAH-ruh-tuh). These poems tell of the struggle between good and evil.

Kathakali dance has musical **accompaniment**. The only instruments used are **percussion** instruments. These include cymbals, drums, and gongs.

India and China are located in Asia.

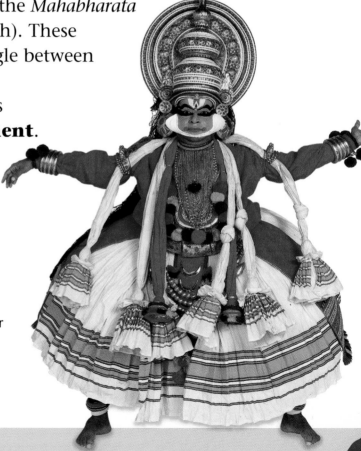

Kathakali dancers wear elaborate costumes.

Kathakali makeup and costumes are colorful. Dancers playing evil characters wear green makeup. Those playing heroes paint their faces red or black. It often takes dancers many hours to put on their makeup since designs are so complicated.

Only men dance the kathakali. The dancers need to be strong and flexible. They work hard to train their bodies.

1 The dancer uses a stem from a coconut leaf to apply makeup.

The heavy headdress is called a kiritam.

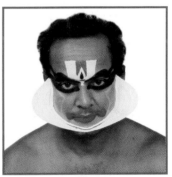

2 The dancer frames his face with white paper to make a chutti.

3 The dancer reddens the whites of his eyes.

Chinese Dragon Dance

Our next stop is China, where we will see one of the world's most exciting dances. The dragon dance is performed in late January or early February to celebrate the Chinese New Year. It is also performed in Chinese communities in many parts of the world.

The dragon dance has been a part of Chinese culture for thousands of years. The dragon is a special creature that many Chinese people believe can bring good luck, wealth, and a long life. Some people also believe that the dragon can protect them from evil and danger.

The head of the dragon costume has animal-like features, such as deer horns and cow ears.

The dragon dance combines dance and **martial arts**. Martial arts are various forms of self-defense. They are based on very old techniques that were developed in China. More than fifty martial artists wear the dragon costume to make the dragon.

The dragon costume consists of a head, a long body, and a tail. It is brightly colored in gold, green, and red. The dragon head and body may weigh more than 200 pounds and stretch to almost 400 feet.

Under the costume, the dancers weave and twist their way through the crowds. The dancers jump, kick, and stomp. They seem to become the dragon!

Martial artists train hard before they perform the dragon dance.

Australia and New Zealand

Aboriginal Dances of Australia

Aboriginal people were the first inhabitants of Australia. Many Aboriginal dances are about the Dreaming, stories that explain how the world was created. The dances originated thousands of years ago, but they are still performed today.

Australian Aboriginal **clans**, or families, have their own stories and dances. Many of these dances are performed for clan members only. Aboriginal people use dance to tell their clan history. A clan's dance might be about a major event, such as the death of a relative. Some dances are only performed by men for men or by women for women.

Australia and New Zealand are located southeast of Asia in the Pacific Ocean.

The didgeridoo is one of the oldest musical instruments.

Aboriginal dancers wear body paint made from white clay, red or yellow stones, or mud. Each pattern and color painted on the body has a special meaning. The dancers also carry traditional objects, such as decorated shields or spears. These special objects add meaning to the dances.

Dances are accompanied by the music of the **didgeridoo** (dihj-uh-ree-DOO). This instrument is made from a hollowed-out log. Musicians make deep musical sounds by continuously blowing into one end of the didgeridoo.

Dancers use natural materials, such as colored earth and rocks, to make body paint.

These male dancers are performing a traditional Aboriginal dance in a theater.

Poi Dance of New Zealand

Now let's visit the Maori (MOW-ree), the **Indigenous** people of New Zealand. The poi (poy) is a traditional dance of Maori women. The word *poi* means "ball." Dancers twirl one to three white balls that are attached to colored string. The balls are filled with reeds and covered with cloth. The dancers move their hands at the same time. They also chant and sing throughout the dance.

The poi dance was created more than 1,000 years ago. The Maori women used the art of poi to help make their hands stronger for weaving. The poi dance is used today to celebrate important events.

poi dancers

These poi dancers are celebrating Waitangi Day, a national holiday in New Zealand.

New Zealand Haka

Visitors to New Zealand are often greeted by a fierce sight. A line of men stand with their eyes bulging and tongues sticking out. They slap their chests, shake their hands, and yell. They are dancing the Haka, the traditional Maori welcome. The only music comes from the dancers' chanting as they move.

People seeing the Haka dance for the first time might find it scary. In fact, Maori warriors danced the Haka to prepare for battle. However, the Haka is most often danced to welcome visitors.

All Blacks Haka

The New Zealand rugby team is known as the All Blacks. The All Blacks perform the Haka before each game to challenge their opponents.

Maori men in traditional dress perform a welcoming Haka.

South America

Tango of Argentina

Our journey now takes us to South America, home of the tango. This dance developed in the late 1800s. It began in Buenos Aires, the capital of Argentina.

At first, tango steps were lively and quick. Over time, people danced the tango to slower musical accompaniment. Many instruments may accompany the tango, including guitar, violin, and flute. The **bandoneon** (bahn-DOH-nee-ahn), a type of **accordion**, is most common.

Argentina is located in South America.

Tango dancers use many difficult footsteps.

This musician in Argentina plays tango music on his bandoneon.

Ballroom dancers often perform the tango wearing formal costumes.

The dramatic tango combines long, slow steps with short, quick ones. Men take the lead in the tango. The man guides the woman into the next move by pressing his hand firmly against her back. The dancers often stop and pose in the middle of a move.

Tango is a type of **ballroom dancing**. There are national and international ballroom dancing events for people of all ages. Someday, ballroom dancing may even be an Olympic sport.

This couple enjoys a tango outside on a crowded street.

North America

Square Dancing of the United States

Swing your partner! **Promenade** right! We are going square dancing in the United States.

The United States is located in North America.

Square dancing is a type of country dancing. Country dancing came from the folk dances of English, Irish, and Scottish immigrants. These dance styles changed over time into the popular forms that are danced today. Square dancing is called a **social dance** because it brings people in the community together.

These young square dancers are entertaining a crowd at a festival.

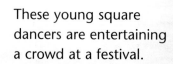

Square Dancing Steps

left arm turn

cross hand swing

promenade

There are specific dance movements, or figures, in square dancing. First, groups of four couples form a square shape. Then a "caller" shouts out the figures in time to the music. The dancers follow the caller's instructions. Couples may take turns joining other couples and doing steps. They might bow to each other or turn in a circle.

Sometimes square dancing is done to lively **bluegrass** music. Bluegrass is traditionally played with stringed instruments, such as fiddles and banjos. Today, square dancing is also done to modern recorded music.

banjo

Africa

The N'cwala Contest of Zambia

Zambia is located in southern Africa.

In Africa, some dances are performed to pounding beats. Many African dances are "call and response" dances. One person leads the movement and others follow. In West Africa, dance is usually accompanied by drums. In East Africa, however, a chorus, or group of singers, usually provides the musical accompaniment.

In southern Africa, the Ngoni (uhn-GOH-nee) people of Zambia hold a yearly festival. This N'cwala (uhn-KWAH-luh) ceremony celebrates a new harvest. One feature of the festival is a dance contest.

These men are in a "call and response" dance.

The balamba drum provides rhythm for some West African dances.

Masks are worn in many African dances. A mask often represents an ancestor of the community.

The dance contest attracts male warriors from twelve Ngoni villages. Each group of warriors competes to show which can best protect the Ngoni chief. The dancers carry shields and wooden sticks, known as N'kholi (uhn-KOH-lee). They wear leopard skins and headdresses made from zebra hair.

Women form a circle around the dancing warriors. They sing and clap loudly. The dancers stamp their feet and wave their weapons. Once the groups have danced, the chief declares the winners. Being a winner is a great honor.

This ten-year-old warrior was the youngest dancer in his group.

Europe

Flamenco of Spain

Welcome to Spain, home to flamenco (fluh-MEHNG-koh) dance. Hundreds of years ago, a group of people called Romanies traveled from India to Spain. Their music and dance is called flamenco. Dancers use flamenco to express their feelings on both joyous and sad occasions.

Flamenco dancing is accompanied by singing called cante (KAHN-tay). The music is played on the guitar. Dancers sometimes use handheld percussion instruments called **castanets** as they dance.

Spain, Ireland, and England are located in Europe.

castanets

Flamenco music is provided by the guitar. Until the 1800s, only singing accompanied the dancing.

Both men and women dance the flamenco.

Flamenco dancing focuses on the feet, arms, and hands. The dancers' feet are never still; they continuously pound the floor. This footwork is known as **zapateado** (zahp-ah-tay-AH-doh). The dancers turn their arms gracefully, sometimes reaching high above their heads. They clap their hands.

As the dance progresses, the dancers move faster and faster. For a moment, they don't seem to be aware of what is happening around them. This moment is called **duende** (DWEN-day), or the trance.

Women flamenco dancers usually wear long, frilly costumes.

Irish Dancing

Irish dancing can be traced back to the 1600s. Dancing masters traveled around Ireland and organized dances. They taught people the steps in return for food and a place to stay.

bodhrán

uillean pipes

Early Irish dance was accompanied by instruments, such as the fiddle and the **uillean** (IHL-awn) **pipes**. Later, people also played the tin whistle and flute. Today, the accordion and bodhrán (BOH-ran) are also used. The bodhrán is a handheld goatskin drum.

The dancers often keep their upper bodies straight and their arms still. They only move their legs.

Morris Dancing of England

Morris dancing began in the small rural villages of England. It's a custom that has lasted for centuries. No one is exactly sure how it started. Some people believe that this lively dancing was used to welcome the spring and chase away the winter.

A few villages have their own local dances. In some Morris dances, they bang sticks on the ground. In others, they wave handkerchiefs in the air. The dancers wear bells strapped to the legs of their costumes.

These Morris dancers bang sticks to welcome the spring.

Dress for Morris Dancing

Flowers decorate the dancers' straw hats.

Dancers wear ribbons or sashes called baldricks around their bodies.

Dancers also wear bells on their legs.

Get Up and Dance

Now you've read about some dances from around the world. Some dances are brought to new lands as people migrate from one place to another. Other dances help keep old traditions alive. Dances can be done in groups or by individuals. Sometimes they are performed in masks and costumes. Some dances have complicated steps, and some require only a flexible body and a good rhythm.

Dance is a way to express who we are and how we feel. You may know of a dance that is unique to your culture, neighborhood, or family. You may even have a dance of your own. Express yourself by dancing your favorite dance!

Glossary

accompaniment	something that goes along with something else
accordion	an instrument with a keyboard on one side and a middle that expands and contracts
ballroom dancing	social dancing in which couples follow a pattern of steps
bandoneon	a type of accordion used in tango music
bluegrass	traditional style of music with stringed instruments, such as fiddles and banjos
castanets	handheld percussion instruments
clans	groups of people with a common ancestor, like families
didgeridoo	a musical instrument from Australia that is made from a hollowed-out log
duende	the trance flamenco dancers may experience
Indigenous	first inhabitants of an area
martial arts	forms of self-defense, such as karate or kung fu
percussion	instruments that produce a sound after being struck
promenade	dance step in square dancing where a couple marches together in a circle
social dance	dance that brings people in the community together
uillean pipes	an Irish instrument made of a bag, bellows, and pipes
zapateado	the footwork in flamenco dancing

Index